CAFÉ CULTURE EVANGELISM

"Come, all who are thirsty, come to the waters"
ISAIAH 55:1

SOLAS
CENTRE FOR PUBLIC CHRISTIANITY

David Robertson
Edited by David J. Randall & Thomas. J. Courtney

SOLAS - Centre for Public Christianity
Swan House,
2 Explorer Road,
Dundee Technology Park,
Dundee, DD2 1DX
Scotland, U.K.
Email: enquiries@solas-cpc.org
Web: www.solas-cpc.org

ISBN (paperback): 978-0-9930832-0-4
ISBN (kindle): 978-0-9930832-1-1
ISBN (ePub): 978-0-9930832-2-8

Second edition. Printed in Great Britain.

Cover photo: Anders Skjærseth

This manual is based on a presentation by David Robertson, Director of Solas (Centre for Public Christianity), Dundee, Scotland; some of his personal comments and illustrations are included in grey-boxes.

Contents

Preface

Solas, as a Centre for *Public* Christianity, wants to encourage the church in its task of presenting the gospel in a persuasive way in its own cultural context. We cannot assume that a twenty-first century post-everything generation will come through our doors seeking to know more about God. That may have happened in centuries past, but in this generation (and probably in the foreseeable future) the church needs to get out into the streets of each local community, with prayer for the Lord's direction, guidance and wisdom. That is the aim of this Quench booklet – to help equip the church to carry out periodic Quench events.

Quench events are designed to reach twenty-first century people in their own cultural contexts through non-threatening, relaxed and relevant events. They can (and should) be designed to reach into all segments of society, whether in pubs, cafes, local auditoriums or church halls.

This is not a simple task. It requires much prayer, thought and boldness to engage people in their own surroundings, but most people (friends, colleagues, family members, neighbours) will at least listen to a reasonable presentation of the gospel. To make that presentation requires an understanding of the society in which the church exists. Jesus spoke with people on their level, as did the apostle Paul. The church of the twenty-first century must learn to do the same.

Of course, whether anyone accepts and makes personal the good news of Jesus Christ depends upon God's work in his/her heart. It is the Holy Spirit who brings people to Jesus. The task of the messenger of the good news is to listen actively, and to communicate in a persuasive, clear, non-combative manner to the person engaged in conversation.

We hope and pray that this booklet will help and equip the messengers of many churches and groups to prepare and implement Quench events, where the gospel can be communicated, shared, questioned, debated, pondered and discussed, in an open, non-hostile atmosphere.

Dr Thomas J. Courtney,
European Co-ordinator & Assistant Director
Solas, (Centre for Public Christianity)

Dr Gordon Wilson,
Chairman, Board of Directors
Solas, (Centre for Public Christianity)

Chapter 1

Why Bother?

The reason for reasoning

Good news for thirsty people

When people are thirsty they want something to drink to quench that thirst.

We believe that people are spiritually thirsty and that we have the means to quench that thirst – the good news of the gospel of Jesus Christ who came to this earth, lived, performed miracles, taught, died on the cross for our sins, rose from the dead, ascended into heaven and is going to come again.

The trouble is that for most people, that's just religious talk and it doesn't make sense to them. They are happy for us to believe it but it's a different matter if we say that it's good news for them and

1

that they need to hear and respond to it.

This manual is about how we communicate the Good News in the context of our particular cultures so that people can understand the message and have the option of refusing or accepting it. We are trying to communicate with people who are unlikely to ever go near a church. We want to remove the barriers that would prevent them from considering Christianity. We are trying to challenge their world views, in which they are often very comfortable; above all, we are trying to communicate and speak about Jesus Christ.

In short, the purpose of Quench is to attempt to lead thirsty people to the One who can quench their thirst. Jesus said, "If anyone is thirsty, let him come to me and drink" (John 7:37).

Depending on the Holy Spirit

Of course we believe that it's ultimately the Holy Spirit who initiates this and works in people's lives. Paul wrote about how he had planted the seed of the gospel and others had watered it, but it was God who made it grow (1 Corinthians 3:6).

Some Christians question the idea of "reasoning" with people (apologetics or what we call persuasive evangelism); they think we should "just tell them about Jesus". This may sound very spiritual, but it is not biblical. In Acts we find Paul, Luke, Barnabas, Mark and the other apostles reasoning:

- They went from house to house reasoning

- They stood up in the synagogue and reasoned

- Paul reasoned with the Athenians, pointing to their idols, quoting their poets, and so on (Acts 17).

This is what we need to do. Of course, we depend on the work of the Holy Spirit, but the Spirit normally works through our minds.

We're all philosophers!

One of the difficulties in our society is that we compartmentalize people, as if some people are practical, some are spiritual and others are academic. Actually, we all have a philosophy, a way of thinking, which influences and determines how we live:

- My fifteen year old daughter is a philosopher
- Ten year old kids in our housing schemes are philosophers
- Academics in the universities are philosophers
- Hairdressers and taxi drivers are philosophers.

We don't need to get people interested in philosophy. Rather, we need to get people to think about what their philosophy is. Most people have an assumed philosophy which they don't really think about:

- In our European culture, for example, most people would say, *"We believe in equality for everyone"*. But what does that mean? How does that work out?
- In other cultures, people might instinctively believe that death is not the end of our existence. What does that mean? How does that work out?

Cultures have mini-cultures within them. In the UK, many people don't regard thinking as a way to approach life. Their assumption is that that's for some people – "intellectuals" – whereas they would claim that they just get on with living their lives without thinking too much about things. But behind this is an underlying philosophy:

- Some people say what the rich man said in Jesus' parable: *"Eat, drink and be merry for tomorrow we die"* (Luke 12:19).

- Others say we just can't know the meaning of life so there's no point even thinking about it.

But all of that is thinking. All of that is a philosophical point of view.

Communicating in a post-Christian culture

Europe today is post-Christian. We're not in the Greco / Roman / Pagan world that was pre-Christian. We are post-Christian. We may be reverting to a Greco / Roman / Pagan worldview but it is a new post–(not pre–)Christian world.

At the end of the "Dark Ages" many people thought the Word of God couldn't be communicated because people couldn't read or write. The printing press hadn't been invented, and the church's message was "owned" by scholars who (in effect) told people what they should believe. Many people went through religious rituals without understanding; they just got on with life, which was sometimes a struggle for survival. At the time of the Reformation remarkable things happened, such as the invention of printing. All of the Reformed churches in Europe – Lutheran, Calvinist, Anglican – believed that education was very important because they wanted to encourage people to think for themselves.

Christianity rejects the view that so long as people have some money and are entertained, that's all that is needed. The gospel says to everyone – ploughboy, factory worker or academic – you need to think and you need to know about Jesus Christ.

We need to know *how* to communicate that. We are not saying in this course that Quench (café evangelism) is the only way or the best way to do it. But it is *part* of *a* way within most of our cultures. Café culture is very strong across most of Europe and it presents an open door to meet people in the marketplace.

People need people

Some people might agree with all of this and go on to say that we should simply communicate the message through our church services and meetings, through the internet and books.

However, although these are obviously wonderful means of communication, most communication still needs to be person-to-person. If a salesman tried to sell you a hair product that he claimed would give you wonderful flowing locks – and then you noticed that he was bald – you wouldn't be impressed! You'd say that his words were denied by his appearance. In communicating the gospel of Jesus Christ our lives and our actions need to match our words.

"I remember an atheist, a lovely guy who was a musician (he even wrote a piece of music against me). He was very hostile to what I was saying. He did become a Christian. You can read about it in *The Dawkins Letters*. I put it in as an extra chapter. He commented later that, as he read over numerous e-mails and letters that I had

> sent him, 'What struck me was not the words of David
> Robertson, but the word of God' "

"The Word became flesh" (John 1,14)

Human beings are made in the image of God:

- We are logical – we can think

- We are spiritual – we can feel

- We are moral – we can choose right and wrong.

The best way of communicating truth is for human beings to talk
to one another. To reach us, speak to us and save us, God himself
in Jesus Christ became a human being. A boy once asked his father,
"Why did Jesus become a human being? Why didn't he just shout
from heaven?" The father pointed to an ant hill and said, "Look at
these ants scurrying around down there? If I wanted to warn them
that their ant hill is about to be destroyed, how could I do that?"
The boy got the point – by becoming an ant. As John wrote in the
first chapter of his Gospel, Jesus made his dwelling among us (John
1:14). He reconnects us to the Father; he gives us living water. He is
the living water.

"You are the body of Christ" (1 Cor. 12:27)

Good news is for sharing – and God works through human beings.
Clearly, he can and does communicate in other ways; for example,
some Muslims have become Christians because of dreams they had.

But normally God communicates through people. It's not enough for a church to hang up a sign saying, "All non-Christians welcome here". That would be like a fisherman hanging up a sign saying, "All fish welcome here". You have to go out and fish! What this course is about is helping, enabling and equipping ourselves to go out into the marketplace and communicate the gospel person to person.

Now that Jesus is not here physically, he wants to work through his people. He sends his Spirit into his people so that we can communicate the good news of what he has done. The best way has always been person to person. We seek to communicate the good news in Quench-type events because God has sent his Son, and through the Holy Spirit some of us have become believers. Obviously this is not the only way to communicate the gospel but the present popularity of European café culture presents an open door in many places.

The Word uses the Word

Another reason for doing this kind of outreach stems from what we are trying to communicate.

We don't want people to get the message that we merely want more people to come to our churches ("become like us", "join our club"). Rather, we want to go further and communicate the message of Jesus Christ.

We don't need to make the Bible relevant. It already is relevant. All we want to do is communicate the message of the Bible to people in their context. It is communicated by individuals to other individuals or groups. That's our purpose.

Questions for further study, discussion and action

- In your cultural context how does the thirst (discussed in this chapter) manifest itself?

- What would you say to someone who said, "But I don't feel thirsty"?

- How would you answer the man who told William Carey, the great Baptist missionary, that if God wants to convert people, he doesn't need any help from us?

- What do you make of the assertion that everyone is a philosopher? Can you name three or four predominant philosophies of the people in your cultural context?

- What are three or four ways in which you could show that the Bible *"is relevant"* in your context?

Chapter 2

What is Café Culture?

Pub, clubs and cafes

All the lonely people

John Donne famously said, "No man is an island" but some people like to think we can live on our own. Western culture has developed such privatized lifestyles:

- at home you can go into your own room and have your own internet and facebook friends; once the dining room, kitchen and living room were the key rooms, but in many new homes it is the bedroom that is the key room, and not just at bedtime!

- at work you can operate in an isolated booth.

- now you can even shop without having personal contact with people.

As a result it is now more than ever possible for people to be loners. That's maybe why in our cities you see so many people who look very lonely. The Beatles sang (in *Eleanor Rigby*), about all the lonely people, "Nobody knows. Nobody cares." Many people in our society feel that.

The need to belong

The problem is that that is not how human beings are made. We are wired to be sociable beings. We want company. We want real friends. We want real community. Despite the undermining of the family in so much of our culture, the vast majority of people still want to belong to real families.

So, we seek out ways in which we can join, ways in which we can belong. In school, that might mean belonging to a group or gang; later it might mean churches, social clubs, the golf club.

For many people, most of their acquaintances are colleagues at work. In traditional Scottish society and in much of the rest of the UK, particularly in urban areas, the pub has been the focus for much of that. Men would go out to the pub, sometimes every night, just for company. Cafés in Spain, even in small towns and especially in large cities, are filled with repeat customers who get together purely for social reasons. *"Tapear"* (to eat tapas) has become an action-verb signifying getting together with a bunch of people just for company. And once a group finds an available table, that table is theirs until closing-time or until they decide to leave. No café/bar will ask them to leave because others are waiting.

Café culture

Recently in Britain we've moved closer to what might be called a European-style café culture. In Dundee, even in February (and it's cold here in February) you can go to the city centre and see people sitting outside in the freezing cold, having a drink or a coffee. Why? It's partly because they're banned from smoking inside, but also because the whole café culture has grown more and more. It seems as though every month there are new coffee shops opening up.

Café culture is people meeting people. You don't pay £3 for a cup of coffee that you could make at home for a fraction of the cost just because you like to sit in the environment. People want to be with people in a relaxed atmosphere where no one is host or hostess; all are equal.

Some may think that hot, sunny places are more relevant places to have cafés. In Spain, for example, the fact that people eat at ridiculous hours (for British people!) is wonderful. There's no hurry. This is not, "get them through as quick as you can; feed them, get them out". Cafés are indeed about food and drink, but food and drink are about humanity and companionship. Perish the day when in Spain, Italy, Greece or Germany, people are sitting in their little rooms with all their technology, never going out, not sitting on the streets, not sitting around talking, discussing, arguing. All over the place, people like to go out. They like to eat, they like to drink together. Eating and drinking together becomes an event and not simply a necessity for food and drink.

In Scotland, we've just been catching up with that, but it's developing throughout Europe, including central and eastern Europe – the opportunity to meet and to share with people, to eat and to drink together and to talk about different things.

This European café culture provides the church with a great opportunity.

Once, in many British pubs, all you could hear was music; you didn't get a chance to talk or think. But in Britain pubs now have wide-screen TVs so that people can go and watch football. This attracts people and they will share the experience together and talk about it.

There are many opportunities for people to sit down and talk. And, interestingly, there's a move towards having cafés that have public events within them. For example, there's the *Café Scientifique*, where a speaker will come and discuss an idea from a scientific perspective. People will sit and listen and talk about it. Sceptics in the Pub is another, and there's live music. Everybody thought live music was going to die down, but there has been a significant increase in live music being done in small venues like cafés and pubs. Food, drink, ideas, music and creativity – it's a potent mix waiting for the final ingredient – the gospel!

Marketplace for ideas

Cafés are marketplaces for ideas. Consider Acts 17. There was a marketplace there. The Epicurean and Stoic philosophers gathered round to discuss the latest ideas. We tend to think our marketplace for ideas is the internet or television, but consider how television news has changed. Twenty years ago you would have had hour-long programmes where people would discuss things for five or ten minutes. Now, you get news snippets that may only last 60 seconds.

There is not much analysis or discussion and it's often very limited and very controlled. But when you're talking to other human beings, you have an opportunity just to discuss ideas, share thoughts, reflect on perspectives.

In America *The White Horse Inn* is a discussion programme for Christian theology and Bible application. It is named after the White Horse Inn in Cambridge which is where many of the English and continental Reformers would gather to discuss philosophy, science and the Bible. Even with limited transport and communications, people from Geneva, Frankfurt, Paris, Edinburgh, London would criss-cross all the time. Patrick Hamilton from St Andrews went across to Germany and founded the University of Marburg there, a fruit of this cross-fertilisation of cultures, discussing ideas and talking with people.

We have a similar opportunity today. We are blessed with wonderful means of communication. At the time of the Reformation they had the printing press. We have the internet as well as the printing press, but we still need to get together to talk about things and to share things because people have different ideas and most people enjoy the opportunity to express their thoughts and ideas.

There is a *Google* and *Wikipedia* view of knowledge – the idea that you can just click and find out what you want to know. But when you click on *Wikipedia*, you only find out what someone else is telling you and quite often you'll only find just what you wanted in order to reinforce your own prejudice. It doesn't contradict you. If you are discussing things with other people, however, they can contradict you; they can make you think.

Google once suggested that their aim was to do away with people's memory. People wouldn't need memory – they would have Google! But that is to take away our humanity. Our humanity enables us to remember things, to think about things and to process things. We are far more complex and complicated than any computer system. And again, part of what we're doing in Quench is recognizing people's humanity and encouraging them to think.

> "Let me put it this way. Sometimes I have to confess I have texted my wife in the house. We don't live in a mansion, but I've done that and she's done that to me. Suppose we all sat round a table having coffee with our smart-phones and all we did was text one another. What a weird picture: four people sitting at a table, able to look at each other but looking at their phones, sending each other messages! Put the phone away! Look someone in the eye. Talk to them. That gives a connectivity, a community and a creativity which is absolutely fantastic for the gospel."

Coffee, community and creativity

So it's not just a marketplace for ideas. The second thing is that it is about community and creativity. Within the church, for example, we talk about learning the Bible. How do you learn the Bible? You can read it; you can think about it for yourself; you can digest other external sources – books and commentaries and so on. But the best way of learning the Bible is in community.

The Scottish theologian, Donald MacLeod, was once asked where he got his theology. He replied that he didn't get it in seminary but from years of sitting in house fellowships with old elders hearing them discuss the gospel and the Bible and argue about it. That is, in a sense, what we are trying to do.

Cafés encourage that community and also the creativity. Some people like talking. Others sit and draw. Some people like music. Others are just incredibly good at connecting and making people feel loved.

Western culture is largely individualistic with a strong emphasis on personal freedom, choice and democracy. These things derive from a biblical view of humanity and biblical Christianity (see Vishal Mangalwadi's *The Book that Made Your World*). But as we've moved away from this creative freedom of individuals and groups, we have ended up with a situation where the State has replaced God and become more and more restrictive. This is seen especially in news content, which is often determined by advertisers, by money or by politicians who like to have control. That seemed to be the way things were going, but with the advent of the internet, we have a renewed opportunity to question.

The atheist, Carl Sagan, in his book *Pale Blue Dot*, said that we must not lose the ability to reason and to question those in authority. From our different perspective we too want to cause people to question. The trouble is that when you're sitting at a computer and interacting with your internet group all you do is reaffirm one another. You find the bits on the internet that suit you and you continue in that way. There isn't any heart-to-heart dialogue.

So now we're coming back to the whole café culture idea. In such a context we are saying, "Let's talk about this; let's meet with people we don't agree with". It is enjoyable and educative to listen to people who profoundly disagree with us, being able to question them and be questioned by them – rather than having a bunch of people who blandly say, "Yeah, yeah, we agree, we agree".

We've thought about how news is communicated.

How do we discuss it? Can we question our leaders? Can we question what we're taught in schools? Can we question what we're told to say in exams in order to pass them? Can we question who we are? Can we question the church? Can we question the Bible?

Yes, we can and café culture is a great context in which to do it.

Questions for further study, discussion and action

- Do you agree that many people today feel lonely? If so, how is that manifested in your culture?

- Does the 'café culture' described in this chapter share any similarities with your culture? If so, what are they? If not, how is it different?

- In what ways could you use the principles of 'café culture' to share the good news in your cultural context?

Chapter 3

Outreach in Café Culture

Having considered the theory and background of café culture, we come now to the question of how we put it into practice. Here we reflect on some areas/ways in which this can be done.

Church coffee shops

If a church has its own building it can hold a coffee shop within that building.

Many church buildings were designed to be opened only on a Sunday. They may be open for other reasons during the week nowadays, but why not have a coffee shop in your church?

There can be problems with that. There is the danger, for example, that it just becomes part of the Christian sub-culture and the only people who come to it are people who already come to your church. That has the disadvantage of taking them away from other contexts where they meet non-Christians.

But there are circumstances in which it can be done.

If your church is on a main street where many people walk *past* and you want them to walk *in*, you might set up a coffee shop. It would need it to be a proper coffee shop:

- With good quality coffee! *Get a proper coffee machine*
- With a pleasant and attractive atmosphere – *not just a table and a couple of wooden chairs*
- Possibly with a bookstall *(unobtrusive)*
- With relaxing music
- With nice décor

This approach has great potential, especially for churches in good situations, with suitable premises, enough volunteers – and preferably enough money to hire someone to make sure it is run professionally. Maybe it could be self-funding. Just make sure it's run properly.

On a lesser scale, you could have coffee mornings and so on. This has often been done as a fundraiser, but you can make use of your premises to provide that kind of café-type atmosphere.

"I know one church that, after enquiring about this café evangelism, asked me to come and do a couple of events for them. I responded by giving them ten principles that we would operate on and told them to come back to me in a year. When they had done them for a year, I agreed to go. They had been creative and, instead of holding a caf on a Friday or Saturday night, or midweek, they did it for their Sunday evening service. Once a month they put tables and chairs into the church and had someone come and give a twenty minute talk usually the minister but also other people. They advertised it. They served really good coffee and even better coffee cake and people were able to text in questions or write them down. The next 40 minutes to an hour was spent discussing the questions. They saw their evening service quadruple, with lots of Christians bringing along non-Christian friends. That's just one example of the kind of thing you can do. You can base it in your own church building."

Your local coffee shop

Another approach is to go regularly to your local coffee shop – whether part of a chain (Starbucks, Costa, etc) or independent – to meet with people there, individually or in a small group, to simply talk together about the gospel. It's not a case of artificially staging some kind of mini-drama in order to reach people! But being in a public place conversing with someone can have an impact.

Another possibility is that a small group Bible Study – for example, a group of mums who have a morning meeting – might decide to meet at the local coffee shop instead of meeting on church premises. They sit at a table, get out their Bibles, do their study, buy coffee there, talk to people. Coffee shops can be used for normal small group studies.

"One lady who came to our church was very interested and wanted to discuss bits of the Bible. We went to a local coffee shop and there wasn't much music it was pretty quiet. Half a dozen tables had people sitting round having coffee. I, of course, have a very quiet, dulcet voice but she was a bit louder. We were discussing the Old Testament and she said to me, 'David, I just don't get the Old Testament. It just seems like God takes the Israelites and he blesses them. Then they screw up and then he punishes them and then they cry for help and he blesses them again and calls them back. And then they screw up and cry for help again. It just goes on for ever.' I laughed because by then the whole shop was listening to me as I gave an explanation of covenant theology, the Israelites, the current day situation and how it all applies to us today. When I thought about it later I realized that I didn't mean to evangelise the whole coffee shop but it happened, spontaneously, by accident if you like.

"Sometimes it doesn't go so well. A friend and I were once sitting in a coffee shop, talking about how we bear witness to Christ, and before we left a man came up to us and swore at us. He accused us of being *God-botherers,* and so on. He'd listened in to our whole conversation."

There may be people who are interested in Christianity but who are not yet ready to do an *Alpha* or *Christianity Explored* course, but they do want to discuss things. So you might say, *"Listen guys. Let's meet up at eleven o' clock and we'll do that."*

There's a Scottish phrase: *"the talk o' the steamie"*. The steamie was the launderette, which was another meeting place. When people didn't have washing machines in their own houses, apartments or flats, they would take their washing to the launderette. While they were waiting for their washing to dry, they would sit with people, reading or talking. In a local community, particularly in an industrialized urban context, people would be saying things like, "Did you hear what's happening to so-and-so?" They would talk about anything – local gossip, new royal baby, football. Our aim is for the gospel to be the talk of the "steamie" so that people are talking about the good news in natural contexts. On buses, restaurants and café people talk about football; we want to hear people talking about Jesus.

> "Let me give you another example. My son, while he was still here in Dundee, before he came to the morning service, broke all my Sabbatarian principles by going with his friends who came to church with him, to have a bacon roll and a coffee in a coffee shop just down the road from the church. They would talk and then pray together before they left to come to church. It's a great idea, a great witness."

'Open Mic' evangelism

We have run Quench events where we've had someone come and speak for about twenty minutes. Usually the café is not exclusively ours; other people are coming in and getting their coffee. Someone speaking for twenty minutes with a microphone gets people's attention and provokes questions. If there will be an opportunity for questions, it's best to have a chairperson who ensures an orderly event.

What's happening there is that people are going in for a coffee and they're hearing a talk. Some people may have come for that specific reason, whereas others just happen to be there. Just be fully aware that in doing so you are opening yourself up to questions, to ridicule and so on.

These are some of the Quench events that we have organised – events within cafes (obviously with the permission of the café owner) that are organized specifically to provoke interest in the gospel.

Literature, art and music

Literature

Many coffee shops are also bookshops or are situated within book-shops. Bookshops will usually love the idea of someone coming in to give a talk about a book. For example, we had someone come and give a lecture on Philip Pullman's atheist children's trilogy. Some-times you could discuss a particular Christian book, but usually it is better to take a popular book that's well known in the secular arena, and give a public talk about it.

The Hobbit is an example of a popular book, written from a Christian context. You could do classics or contemporary books, current affairs, poetry, and so on. Surely every city in Europe will have a group of people who will be interested in hearing a talk on Dostoyevsky? Robert Burns, the Scottish poet, is still a saint in Russia. You could use some of the great writers, all different kinds of writers, in different cultures and different contexts.

Art

It's an interesting thing that in art galleries and museums, the 16th, 17th, 18th and 19th century galleries are crowded with people but in the 20th century gallery you could have enough space for a game of football because people aren't really interested. The only people who are really interested in a lot of contemporary art are the artists themselves, the very limited art world or private art collectors who think they are going to make a lot of money out of buying a cow broiled in formaldehyde!

Ninety percent of these earlier paintings are associated in some way with the Bible and Christianity. So you could have an art café, with someone speaking about art, showing paintings and using art to communicate the gospel.

We don't want to despise contemporary art either – there are many questions and gospel opportunities raised within that context as well. Hans Rookmaaker's *Modern Art and the Death of a Culture* is a helpful introduction to how modern contemporary art has developed. You could have someone base a series of talks around the way in which modern art has developed and so on. Or you could arrange a series of lectures on Picasso or Kandinsky; you don't actually need to be an art expert to do that.

Another approach in the café context is to get local artists to display their work and then have a discussion about art. After all, everybody recognizes art. The "apologetic of beauty" is phenomenally important. And in Europe of all places! How could you be in Italy and not talk about art? How could you be in Spain and not talk about art? How could you be in Athens and not talk about art? Even Edinburgh? Dundee? London? Art is everywhere and art has deeply influenced every culture. Figure out how and use it as an opening for the gospel.

Music

Music is also everywhere, and there are various ways in which it can be used. You might have a well-known musician who is a Christian come and talk about their work or you could organize an acoustic café where people come and perform and even talk about their music.

Jazz cafés work well. We had a jazz band once and, although the concert in church wasn't so good, they attracted much attention in the café down the road. The café was half full when we started, but by the time we had finished it was packed to the door. People invited their friends via Facebook and text message. There was a wonderful atmosphere and a great opportunity.

You could have cafés about music where someone gives a talk on the music, or where someone just plays the music. There is tremendous scope in that.

Another approach would be that of having a group of musicians come and play, and then saying that they would be doing a concert in the church the following night. You could have the musicians simply talk about what they were doing. You could have a bookstall; you could have a chairperson who introduces it and explains why you're doing what you're doing: "We're from the church up the road. We believe that music is a gift from God".

The best songs generally reflect biblical themes – questions of suffering, love, pain, and so on. You'll also find scope in the classical tradition. How can you play Bach, Beethoven or Mozart without bringing in some aspect of Christianity? Music can be a stepping-stone to communicating the gospel.

It's a mistake to think that if you've had an event and you haven't given the four points of the gospel, you've failed. And please don't make the mistake of having music and at the end saying, "Oh, by the way, believe in Jesus", and then go. You need to think in a broader context. You need to think in terms of follow-up. And remember – it's still about person-to-person contact. You will need Christians to be there, not sitting in a Christian huddle, but sitting with people at tables, getting to know people and talking to people – overcoming some of the personal barriers.

Music can directly communicate the gospel, it can allude to the gospel, or it can simply be a kind of pre-evangelism, a point of contact with people so that you will eventually be able to communicate the gospel. Some people might say, "But you're just entertaining people." To which the response would surely have to be Robert Murray McCheyne's "My aim is to entertain them into the kingdom"! The apologetic of music, as with all of the arts, is that all awareness of beauty ultimately derives from the beautiful One, God himself.

History and politics

We've considered literature, art and music. Think also about history. Every community in Europe has a Christian history. It's amazing in our postmodern a-historical culture that many people still want to know history, so use history in that context.

You can also use politics. That's a bit more precarious but you can certainly use politics. We've done, for example, a café event on economics, on capitalism – the crisis of capitalism and what's involved with that.

Questions for further study, discussion and action

- Would it be possible/desirable to run a coffee shop in your church building? Advantages? Disadvantages?

- Can you identify the coffee shops in your locality? Which ones could work for a Quench event? Why?

- In order to achieve more exposure in your community, could any of your small groups hold their meetings in a coffee shop instead of on church premises?

- Think out ways in which (a) literature, (b) art and (c) music could become points of contact in your cultural setting.

Chapter 4

How do we organize events

Prayer, preparation and publicity

The organization of events will vary according to circumstances, but the basic principles are the same. There are several things to be considered in laying the groundwork for your outreach.

Prayer

This first and most important thing is prayer. If you are going to do this, don't decide to do it and work out everything and then get prayer backing. Rather, begin with prayer. Even recruit a team of prayer warriors and keep them informed of every step, every obstacle, every success. If you have the desire to communicate the gospel in a public marketplace, ask the Lord where would be best, who might help, who could speak, and so on. Make all of this a matter of prayer. That is crucial before, during and after the event.

Venue

The second thing you need to think about is the venue. Where are you going to do it? This will involve some research – which is a pleasant aspect of preparation – you have to visit the coffee shops and pubs in your area! Obviously, if you're a regular customer in a place, it will be easier to get permission. When the manager knows who you are, it's easier to say, "Would it be possible to do something in here on Monday evening at 7 o'clock?"

In each one, have a look round and think about whether it would be suitable for your purposes. Look at it in terms of acoustics, how busy it is, etc. For example, if it's a Starbucks in a central railway station, you might as well forget it – you're not going to get permission to do anything there. They don't need the custom and in fact they would be scared that you might chase away customers!

Think also about numbers. People get very obsessed about numbers. You're probably not going to have coffee shop evangelism with 200 people, but if you hire a venue for 70 or 80 people and only 5 turn up, that doesn't look good. So think about the size of the venue and if possible think through a workable scenario should only ten come to the event in a venue that is suitable for 70 or 80.

Another thing about preparation is to encourage churches to work together with other churches in which they have confidence, believers who share the same basic understanding of the Scriptures and the fundamentals of the Christian faith. Secondary issues don't matter for this type of event but primary issues do matter.

Speaker

A key aspect of organizing a Quench event is careful consideration of the person you will invite to speak, the musician(s), artist(s), etc. Not everyone who is a good writer is a good speaker. Not everyone who is a good preacher is a good speaker in this kind of context because the key thing here is question-and-answer. The speaker needs to give the audience something to bite into, even provoke them, and then let them fire questions. So the selection of the speaker is crucial because some people can stand up and give a lecture but when it comes to questions they get torn to pieces. You may only get one shot at this and you need to make sure that the person you've got knows what s/he is doing. This is not for rookies. Solas is helping to train people; maybe we can help you find people.

Also, in looking for speakers, you need to look for people who know what they're talking about. On the one hand, we don't want an aggressive, in-your-face, yelling-at-people style; on the other hand, neither do we want them to be completely bland (the kind of 'wet' Christian who just says, "Oh yes, you're right"). They need to be confident – able to discuss, provoke, stimulate, disagree and communicate the truth through it all.

It is also a good idea to have a chairperson for the event. Perhaps someone connected with your church could do this. You can also do debates in these kinds of contexts and if it's a debate, you definitely need a neutral chairperson. But in general it's a good idea to have someone chair the event.

You also need to have in the room some Christians who know what they're doing. If the speaker takes apart the defeater beliefs that people have, he wants to be able to point to you and people from your church and say to his hearers, "If you want to meet Jesus, talk to them or go to their church on Sunday; you'll meet Jesus."

Your 'audience'

After thinking about your speaker and your place, think about the people you are aiming for? That will help you determine when to hold the event. For example, you would not hold an event for students at eight o'clock in the morning! You would not hold an event aimed at elderly people that started at nine or ten o'clock at night. And don't try to reach men on an evening when the local football team has a European Champions League Match.

Practicalities

There are other aspects of preparation. It is important to make sure that you have good sound equipment that is working. It doesn't need to be flashy, especially if it's just a talk in a small room. It's best if you can use a radio mic. If you can't do that, a free-standing mic is fine but make sure your speaker knows how to use it. If there are questions, then you need to have a roving mic to be able to pick up questions. You also need to think about issues of placement:

- Where will the person stand?
- Where will the microphones and sound system be placed?
- Easy access? Easy departure?

- Place to mingle afterwards?

Also – think about the coffee. In one English city, the Pentecostal church and the Presbyterian church got together and hired a Costa café. Costa's was given over to them exclusively, the Costa staff were there, people paid £2 and for that they got a coffee. They could buy cakes and/or another coffee. Over 100 tickets were sold, the place was absolutely packed and it worked very well.

Another approach is for the coffee shop to agree to give you a microphone, some tables and so on. There may be other people who are coming in just to have coffee.

> "One lady in a Scottish city came in, bought her panini and cappuccino and sat down. When the speaker started, the look on her face said, 'Oh, no! I've walked into a religious meeting!' But she was from Aberdeen(!) She said, 'There's no way I'm walking out of here without eating my panini and drinking my coffee.' So she tried to demonstrate that she wasn't listening which is hard to do (when you try not to listen to someone, it's impossible!) she heard every word! By the end she was down at the front, asking questions."

You need to act as a group in this project, not on your own. At least ensure that you have some audience – we would suggest at least ten to twenty people. Don't pack the place out with Christians. Another church in England hired a hotel and sold tickets 5 at a time, which included coffee and a cake. It worked well because the organizers didn't allow people in their church to buy a single ticket; they had to buy two, and one had to be for a non-Christian.

This also raises the question of charging. Shouldn't it be a free event? Sometimes this will depend on cultural factors but in many contexts people are suspicious of 'free' events, arguing that there is no such thing as a free lunch! If you sell tickets then those who buy them are more likely to turn up and you have the advantage of knowing what the turn-out is likely to be.

Publicity

Good publicity is very important. You probably have people in your fellowship who are gifted in graphic design. If you don't, you must find people (again, ask us – maybe Solas can help you). A Quench leaflet must have good quality graphics and be well produced – not a simple A4, photocopied on black-and-white. It shouldn't have too much information on it. Things need to stand out. Obviously there's the basic information: the event, the title, the date, time and place (with "All Welcome"). And you need to make sure that the publicity is distributed.

Posters work quite well. We suggest for any event you have A4 posters or possibly larger. You could have A5 leaflets to be distributed at random in your church, out on the streets, elsewhere, and possibly A6 or smaller invitation cards to give to people to invite them to come.

On the day

It is good to meet for prayer beforehand. It is good for you to turn up at the venue at least an hour beforehand. Any equipment should be set up then. If it is a public marketplace, a public café, it's good to hand out leaflets during the day. In one Starbucks event, the speaker was sitting having a coffee and the staff were handing out leaflets to all customers about coming to hear a gospel talk!

Don't worry too much about starting your event precisely on time. The more important thing is that if you tell people it's going to be an hour, you make it an hour. It's better to leave people wanting more rather than wondering when it is going to end, or (worse) wanting to get out! Of course, people can get up and just walk out. They can do that in other contexts too, but here you will have people coming and going during the event. Speakers need to be aware of that; if you are disconcerted by someone getting up and walking out, then you're not going to make a good speaker at one of these events.

You also need to ensure, with the blessing of the manager, that on the day you have people on the door, and perhaps also people out in the street handing out invitations. At the very least you need two people on the door. If it's a ticketed event you certainly need someone on the door, and even with a non-ticketed event, if you have exclusive use of the premises, make sure that there are two people on the door all the time. They can explain what's going on to people who are coming in – *"There's this man giving a talk – get yourself a coffee – you're welcome."* They can also interact with people who leave. *"Are you OK? Would you like more information?"* and so on.

Also on the day, if you have permission, it's good to be able to have either a book table or a table with leaflets which give more information about where people can find out more.

There are some things that your chairperson should be aware of for the question-and-answer session. First of all, he or she should be as fair as possible while insisting that people ask questions and not make speeches. You should encourage open questions. Of course the chairperson should be a confident person who knows what s/he is doing and has a good understanding of people.

If it's a large venue, you will need a couple of people who are prepared to walk around with a hand mic. Alternatively, you could ask people to come up and ask a question at a fixed mic, but this is only necessary if the venue holds a hundred or more.

In most cases, you should not start these events with prayer, singing or a Bible reading. That's not what this is about. You and the organising team have already prayed with the prayer team beforehand and hopefully there are people praying throughout; in some situations, you could have a small group who will go to another room and just pray throughout the whole event. You may have people back at the church praying. However, you shouldn't normally begin this event with public prayer or Bible reading and you certainly wouldn't have singing (unless your talk happens to be on hymn singing and you want to illustrate it!) Your own people need to understand that you are not holding a church service; this is not an assembly of God's people in public worship. Put yourself in the position of people who are coming in off the streets to have a cup of coffee and a wee break when suddenly there's this religious thing going on. You have about sixty seconds to get their attention and make them think about it.

When the event is finished, it is a courtesy to the staff and the owners of the café that you finish on time, thank them and clear out in time; also, that you give them the money that is due to them. If the event is being held in a commercial coffee shop and they are not charging you for the use of it, then you should encourage the people who have come to listen to the talk that they must buy something! Otherwise that creates bad feeling. The café will want to get some trade from it.

Some suggested topics for Quench Events

The following are some pointers that could be tweaked and adapted to your circumstances for use at Quench-type events. Other topics may occur to you. These are given to "prime the pump". Many topics have a short shelf-life as they are in and out of the headlines, but it is good to be alert to whatever is topical and then seek to give a gospel view on it.

1. *Football in the city* – best if you can invite a Christian footballer to speak

2. *Rock/Jazz* in the city

3. *Art in the city* – depending on the city, you could "use" a well-known artist, designer, etc

4. *Music in the city* – a composer, group, or artist could be the topic (Mozart – Vienna; hip-hop or rap – nearly any city in the UK; Bach – nearly any city in Germany, etc)

5. *Sex and the city*

6. *Death and life in the city*

7. *Loneliness in the city*

8. *How do I look?* – self image/body image amongst teenagers and university students

9. *The God Particle*

10. *Science versus religion* – in relation to God's existence

11. *Education and the city*

12. *Modern media:* bane or blessing?

13. *Social media:* good, bad or indifferent?

14. *The God question*

15. *Morality in the workplace*

16. *Where can we find a basis for morality?*

17. Use any controversial, well-marketed, "talk of the town" new film. Develop Quench event around the theme of the film

18. Do the same as 17 using a new novel or non-fiction book – anything in writing from the latest economic, social, or psychological guru or political pundit

19. Poetry reading with discussion of salient points

20. *Video games* – violence, sex and the adolescent mind

21. *Drug addiction and how I became free.* This would need to be a real-life testimony from someone who was strung out on drugs but now living cleanly a life for the Lord

22. *Drug addiction: helping loved ones in danger.* Again, use a real-life testimony from someone who has been there and found success through tough, biblical love

23. *Why* – suffering, pain, dread and darkness turned into dawn – using personal, real-life testimonies

24. *Life after divorce?* More human-interest testimony that speaks of God's victory in real-life situations, found in nearly every cultural context

25. *Only one way?*

26. *Is Man just Matter?*

Follow up, follow through, follow on . . .

Occasionally, after one of these events, someone has come up and said, *"I'd like to become a Christian"*, but that's rare. What is more likely is that there will be people who say things like, *"They're all idiots!"* You may also find that some people will say things like, *"OK, that wasn't what I expected it to be. That was quite interesting. Where do I find out more without going to church?"*

You have to prepare your follow-up very carefully. You should always have information that you can give to anyone who would like to know more. If you have a website you can say, *"Go to this website and you will find out more."* On the Solas website we will be producing video answers to typical questions – you could encourage people to have a look. But also offer personal follow up: *"Were you really interested in that? Would you like to meet for coffee and discuss some more?"* Don't be afraid to invite people to church. Say, *"Look, we're from the church up the road and, if you want to come and find out more, then – no pressure – you don't have to join, just come along and see what we do".*

Often this kind of event is excellent for starting Alpha, Christianity Explored or Life of Jesus courses. Make sure there is follow-up and perhaps think about starting some kind of course with a particular event. Your outreach shouldn't just be a one-off. It's better to do something on a monthly basis or at least every three months, in the same venue, and develop a reputation for the quality of the events you hold.

Question–and–answer

Some advice for the question-and-answer session: the first rule is – *listen to the question!* Listen to what is being asked. Sometimes, just to make sure, ask the person to repeat the question or to explain it a bit more. Sometimes, what you hear is not what they are saying. Take a classic example: "Why is there suffering?" The questioner might not be asking a question at all. It may be an accusation: "There can't be a God because there is suffering". It's more of a statement than a question. On the other hand, the underlying question might be, "Why did my wife just die?" – and that would affect the way in which you would answer. So when someone comes out with a question like, "Why is there suffering?" you need to respond: *"That's a huge question and I am prepared to answer it, but can I ask you first of all why you're asking that question? Are you concerned in general about suffering in the world or is it more personal to you? Feel free to answer or not if you want, but let me know".*

So, in a question-and-answer session, make sure you grasp what the question is.

Secondly, follow Jesus who didn't always answer questions directly. He sometimes broadened the context. We'll come on to this more fully in a later chapter, but if you were asked, "What do you think of homosexuality?" – don't, in our cultural context, answer that question directly with a one-line answer which would satisfy your church leadership. You've got to think about where the questioner is coming from and what is being said.

So, you are listening to what people are saying, you are trying to grasp where they are coming from and you're trying to get them back to basics. They may be asking a question that comes at the end of the sequence of $1+2+3+4+5$ and they're asking about 6. To answer the question, sometimes you have to go back to 1.

The other thing to remember is: answer the question! Don't avoid it or waffle on about different things. If you can't answer a question, say so. It's fine to say, *"I'm sorry I don't know the answer to that."* Sometimes you have to say, *"I'm not really prepared to answer that question"*, either because you don't know enough or because it is entirely irrelevant.

The question-and-answer is the real key because that's where the interaction takes place. Again, for those who are speakers: you must be firm but loving. If you are naturally humorous, use that; sometimes, if you're nervous, you can over-do it, but careful use of humour can lead to people saying, "You're not as bad as we thought you were"!

It's also good when someone asks you a question to answer that person directly as if you were dealing only with them. Ravi Zacharias often does this; he will ask the person to stand, even in an audience of hundreds or thousands, so he can look at their face and talk to them. We are not going to have audiences of hundreds or thousands in coffee shop evangelism, but look at the person. Talk to them. You're not answering for the people around you. You're not answering for your pals. You are not defending yourself. You are talking to that particular person and you may only get one shot.

Using the Bible

Because the Bible is God's Word, it is powerful. In talks and also in question-and-answer sessions, you don't always have to give chapter and verse. For example, "God so loved the world that he gave his only begotten son" – you don't have to say it's John 3:16. Of course you have to know the references; if someone asks where that comes from in the Bible you really should know. But you're not in a church context where people are sitting with Bibles and are able to look it up. You can use Bible phrases and Bible teaching without necessarily telling people that it's from the Bible. That can actually be very, very subversive but it works. It works because it's the Word of God. It's not the Word of God because you pronounce it as the Word of God, or because you say it's from the Bible. It's the Word of God because it is the Word of God.

Often in apologetics and philosophy, people get to a certain point and then stop. They don't point to Christ. Your event has failed if at some point it hasn't pointed to Jesus. They say that all of us are only six links away from being related to everyone else in the world – every question is only two or three links away from being connected to Jesus Christ. But please don't just say, "Jesus is the answer!" You can communicate that by wearing a T-shirt! But you can show them why Jesus is the answer and how Jesus is the answer to their questions.

Having the right attitude

Speakers need to be really careful, because as they address the audience it would be possible to say something that would put people off Christianity for the rest of their days. It's not that you should react by saying, "I'm going to say nothing offensive" – then you could become so bland that you would make Christianity appear boring. What you need to do, without being offensive and provocative, is to be yourself and communicate the truth. Look at the person/people you're talking to and see them as they are – as human beings for whom Christ died, and you long for them to know Jesus. Speak to them as though they were your best friend.

One other thing for speakers: if you are used to doing this, don't get too confident. They say that when you learn to ride a motorbike the most dangerous time is not at the beginning, when you're learning, but when you've passed your test and you think you can do it. You get too cocky and you end up having an accident. Go in knowing that you are not adequate for the task, knowing that it's not about you anyway but that the Lord will enable. That is very important for the speaker.

> "When you are speaking and doing this, don't do what I did one day when I went to a bookshop here in Dundee. It was my third event there and I went in thinking, 'Home territory, this is pretty easy. I've done this many times before.' About halfway through the talk, I was just hit with this thought, 'You complete idiot! What made you think you can do this on your

own!' I was glad to get through it. It wasn't a complete disaster. It went okay, but I can tell you this. When I got home I got on my knees and I said, 'Lord, I'm sorry. I won't do that again'."

For further study, discussion and action

Review the aspects of preparation outlined in this chapter in relation to your own situation:

- prayer
- venue
- speaker
- chairperson
- audience
- practicalities
- publicity
- follow-up

Can you develop a plan of action for each of the aspects mentioned above? Begin now.

Chapter 5

What do I do if . . .

No-one turns up?

One difficulty that can arise is that you organise an event and nobody turns up (or very few people turn up). This is often the dread of event organizers, particularly church leaders: "What if no one turns up?" They haven't sold tickets; they've just done it as an open event, so they go to their congregation and all their friends and say, "We're holding this event. Please come along or the event will be a disaster." This can result in an event where out of 100 people attending, 95 are churchgoers!

In fact, it doesn't really matter if there are only ten people present. The issue is not numbers. Of course it's great if an event is packed, but experience shows that events which are packed out with Christians can be a washout. They just don't work.

Sometimes if things go wrong, they go wrong. You're taking a risk. There is no guaranteed success. You may feel discouraged, but don't let it destroy you or your enthusiasm for café evangelism.

Things turn awkward?

Other things can go wrong. In the question-and-answer time, you can find that there are no questions! That generally happens when it's mostly Christians who are there – although you can avoid that by priming two or three people beforehand to ask questions. Such a stratagem may help the audience to have confidence and encourage them to ask questions. Generally, though, you should have a speaker who provokes questions because a speaker is not someone who is there to give all the answers.

One problem that can arise with questions is that they are asked by the wrong people! At one event in England, a man stood up and asked the speaker if he thought that Richard Dawkins was the antichrist. The man wanted to give his own particular version of Christian prophecy and its effect was to make Christians look absolutely wacky. How do you deal with that? You could have bouncers at the door to go and throw him out, but that would look pretty dramatic! You need a speaker who knows what he's doing. That particular gentleman was just heckling. An able speaker can use heckling to make Christianity look sane rather than insane. You can even get the atheists on your side!

"Once at an event in a coffee shop, the chairman called for questions and a man stood up and opened his shirt to reveal a big letter 'A' on his T-shirt. 'A' stood for atheist. He asked me a question and it was quite aggressive. So I just said to him, 'Do you have the "A" in case you forget?' People started laughing. I answered his question and we bantered back and forth for a bit. It was a wee bit aggressive but you can handle that kind of aggression. On another occasion, I was in Cambridge at a bookshop near the University, and I mentioned that I was quite surprised that the new atheists get very emotional. At that point a man (it turned out that he was a university lecturer) shouted out, 'What do you mean emotional! We don't get emotional! What are you talking about, you idiot!' He was yelling at me, emotionally, for at least 60 seconds if not two minutes, and was only stopped by one of his friends shouting out, 'Shut up and sit down, you fool you've just proved his point!' The guy did shut up, he did sit down, and to be fair to him, at the end, he did come up and apologise to me. He said, 'I kind of handed that to you on a plate, didn't I?' "

If things go wrong, it's important to remember that it's not about you – it's about Jesus.

In any case, we should be cautious about judging whether something has gone wrong. If you are in a meeting with 100 people and every one of them goes away and it makes no difference to any one of them, could that be described as a successful meeting? On the other hand, if you are in a meeting with eight people and one of them becomes a Christian, is that not a fantastic thing?

So do all the preparation, do all the prayer. Make your best effort. Don't be fatalistic or over-optimistic. Do it all but remember that it's all in God's hands and that, if things go wrong, that is in God's hands too.

"Let me give an example of how being robust can work. We had a great event at Queen's University in Belfast. It was packed with about 400 people and it was mainly a question-and-answer session. A man stood up at the back and he was a Goth, dressed in black eyeliner, black nose ring the whole works. He was very aggressive and he asked in a very aggressive Northern Irish accent, 'There are thousands of myths about babies being born on 25 December. Why should we believe your particular one?' My response was (and this is why sometimes it's dangerous to speak off-the-cuff because I just gave the answer that came immediately to my head) which was, 'Sir, you are a prime example of the dangers of Wikipedia.' The whole place burst into applause and laughter and he just glowered at me. I explained, 'There aren't hundreds of myths about babies being born on 25 December. It's all completely wrong.' And I answered his question eventually, but in a fairly aggressive manner. Afterwards, I was signing books and I saw him standing at the back of a queue of about 50 people and he was looking mad. I thought, 'I hope there's no gun underneath that coat'! I was thinking, 'He'll go away. He'll get bored.' But he didn't. He was the very last one. So I stood up, put my hand out to him and said, 'I'm sorry for miscalling you and making fun of you in public.' He just looked at me (I won't use the full range of his language as this is a Christian book) and he said, 'No, you were ******* right. I was such a ******* idiot. To be honest, if you'd given me any of that ******* Christian junk I would have been up and out of here but I was so surprised at your answer I thought I'd stay and listen to the rest of it.' So sometimes these things work."

The sound system isn't working?

Sometimes the technical equipment is awful. Ninety percent of the time, that gets dealt with if you set up beforehand and test it. If the venue is small enough, you can do without a sound system, but it's important that you have somebody there who knows what they are doing technically so they can deal with unexpected issues.

As the events are quite informal, if something doesn't work out particularly well, you can say, "Hang on a minute. We've got something wrong here. Get yourself another coffee while we get it sorted out". Just make sure that someone is present who knows what s/he is doing with the technical equipment.

Except in the very smallest venues, it's advisable to have a microphone and sound system – not least because if the person giving the talk stands up and shouts at people, that comes across as aggressive – which is undesirable.

Some things are beyond your control (like the lights going out); you just have to follow the Scouts' motto – *be prepared*. Think in advance about what a worst case scenario would look like and work hard to avoid it. For example, if a microphone stops working, is a back-up microphone available? Just be prepared as best you can.

A common problem is that the roving mic for questions doesn't work. If that happens, just have the chairperson repeat the question. By the way, if you are a chairperson and someone asks a long question, don't repeat the whole question; just summarise it. That's also a good idea if you are the speaker – summarise the question and ask, *"Is that OK? Is that what you asked?"* That helps to assure clarity of the question.

We want to make a recording?

There are pros and cons about this. Audio recordings can be useful: you can put them on your website, making them available to other people. Video recording can be even better although two problems can arise if you want to video members of the audience:

- One is that, if you're going to video events, you need people who really know what they're doing. You need two cameras, different angles, and so on.

- The other issue is that if you're videoing the audience and you are going to put the result online, you have to be aware that there may be people who wouldn't want their image to be seen in public. You can ask people to sign a disclaimer form, or you can simply tell the audience that you're going to put it online, or make a DVD of it, and if anyone would prefer for their image not to be used, please indicate to us accordingly.

If you are recording, then, when it comes to questions, you have to make sure that the questions can be heard on the video and audio. So the question needs to be either recorded through the mic or repeated by the chairperson.

Generally, recording events can be useful. If you make a video and it turns out to be pretty well rubbish – just don't use it. But at other times, you may come up with real gems that you can use in different contexts. So, in general, if it's feasible, we recommend making at least an audio recording and, if possible, a video.

Questions for further study, discussion and action

- How do you assess the success or otherwise of an event? Think through several things that, should they all occur, would lead you to say that the event was a success. Do the same, describing a mediocre event.

- How would you have dealt with the man who asked if the speaker thought Richard Dawkins is the antichrist? What aspects of your response could you use for any heckler?

- What other difficulties could you anticipate? How will you deal with them?

Chapter 6

Questions people ask

This chapter will not provide you with complete answers to all the possible questions people ask, but we hope it will give you some pointers on how to handle a few of the more typical questions.

The first thing about questions is that you need to work out whether the question is a genuine one or whether it is really an accusation. For example, the question, "Why are you such an idiot?" is not really an enquiry about one's mental health! Some things can be accusations; questions about sexuality and science can often be statements or assertions rather than questions, even though they are expressed in question form. The person handling the questions needs sensitivity and discernment to work out which is which.

The second thing is: where is the question coming from? What is the underlying assumption upon which the question is founded? Sometimes the best approach is not to answer the question directly but to dismantle the underlying assumption because then the question falls.

In this chapter we will consider five general questions which come up frequently.

Hasn't science disproved God?

Deconstructing the question

The first thing you need to do with this question is to look at the assertion behind it and question whether it is valid. Usually this question is asked by people who haven't really thought through the topic.

We are talking about presuppositions. The first thing is that the question is based on a wrong definition of faith. It assumes that faith is belief contrary to, or in spite of, the evidence while science is about empirical proof. So when someone says, "Hasn't science disproved God?" - don't immediately get into answering that particular question. First, ask your own questions:

- *What do you mean by science?*

- *What do you mean by proof?*

- *What do you mean by God?*

Usually someone who asks the question is assuming that human beings came out of the primordial swamp, evolved, became conscious, looked at the stars and the sun, didn't understand what they were seeing and said, "Big shiny thing - must be a god". People are asserting that we attributed natural forces to God. And they assume that, as we become more and more scientific and understand more and more things, the gap left for God shrinks to the point where the only people remaining who believe in God are either evil or ignorant. So when you're answering this question you have to keep all such presuppositions in mind.

Complementarity

It is a mistake to say, "Yes, science and Christianity are opposed and I'm going with God on this one." We need to affirm that Christianity and science go together. Thus you make your own presuppositions clear; you are saying that science and Christianity are not opposed. It's helpful to use Newton, the Royal College of Science, as well as the Puritans and their whole idea that God has created two books - the book of nature (which we observe in science) and the book of revelation (the Bible).

Evolution?

People often want to raise questions and arguments about evolution. It is usually unwise to get into this in the context of coffee shop evangelism. It's better to say to people, *"I'm not prepared at this stage to get into that kind of discussion. Even if macro-evolution turned out to be true, it wouldn't prove that there is no God. That's not the issue. We can talk about that some other time."* Actually, it is often Christians who ask that question; they want an in-house Christian argument – which is not something to be conducted in public.

Richard Dawkins has two points. Point one is that evolution is true, and point two is that because it is true there is no God.

We should go for point two. Point two is not logical. It does not logically follow from point one. It is possible that you could believe in evolution and believe that God did it. That is a logical possibility.

Christians and science

Another good way of dealing with the science question is to point out that there is a significant number of scientists who are Christians. If people have been following atheist websites, they may come up with the assertion that surveys claim that 90% of scientists in North America are atheists. Then what you have to say is, *"I'm sorry, but can you please show me your surveys, because I really doubt that"*. Get some of the basic information that you need if you're going to answer that kind of question. You can name individual scientists (people like John Lennox).

If you want to go along a more philosophical route, you can point out that modern science is based on Christianity. There are many books and resources on this subject, but the simple argument goes like this: the majority of human beings have believed that the universe is chaotic, that it is not ordered. Christians, Muslims and Jews all believe that the universe is ordered, and because it's ordered you can study it. Whenever you do science, you presuppose certain things and these presuppositions are fundamentally theological ones that only make sense in a Christian worldview. A scientist presupposes that there is order and uniformity. That's what the Bible says. We need the philosophical basis of Christianity, or at least of theism, in order to do modern science, because Christianity is based on a worldview of order and uniformity.

Science / scientism

One other thing in answering this question and the presuppositions behind it is that people are not usually saying that science disproves Christianity. In reality they are expressing their own philosophy which is scientism. Scientism is a form of logical positivism which states that we can only know things are true if they can be empirically proved. Logical positivism is the basic presupposition assumed by most people who ask this question about science disproving God, but logical positivism, as a philosophy, has failed. Virtually nobody holds to it – because the statement that we can only know that things are true if we can empirically prove them is itself something that cannot be empirically proved. It is not verifiable. It is self-refuting.

Scientism is a faith. It's a faith that only material things exist. It's a faith that there are only chemicals. It's a faith that everything - love, beauty, truth, everything – can be reduced to chemical reactions. In another form it is called naturalism. It is not a scientific position. To be a naturalist requires a great deal of faith and most of the people who are asking that question are actually just telling you their philosophical position.

In a question-and-answer session, you may not have much time to get into all of this but you should at least be aware of some of these issues.

Remember too that it's always helpful to have a bookstall in the room, or at least to be able to recommend books to people. *God's Undertaker: Has science buried God?* by John Lennox is a classic, and there are numerous others as well. There are also courses that you can use where you can look at the whole interface between Christianity and science.

When you're dealing with this question, your main goal is to undermine the myth – and it is a myth – that Christianity and science are opposed to one another.

The question of suffering

When people ask about suffering, it is wise to assume that they are talking from their hearts as well as their heads. Care is needed in responding to such questions.

The reason why

The questions usually focus around the question, "Why is there suffering in the world?" Answering properly requires at least an introduction to the concept of the Fall.

When this is introduced, people may ask, "But couldn't God have prevented that?" And we can answer, *"Yes, he could. He could have given us a world without pain, sorrow, suffering, broken relationships or cancer. God might have said, 'You can have that if you want it. Do you want it? Yes? OK, I'm going to make you into a chair'. In other words, God could have made us robots"*. You are dealing with the assumption that lies behind the question.

To our atheist friends we can say, *"If, as you believe, there is no God, it's tough!"* My favourite Dawkins quotation is from The Blind Watchmaker where he says that the universe has precisely the qualities that we would expect if there is no God; it is cold, indifferent, pitiless – no mercy, no love, etc. That's the world you live in if there is no God. Be consistent with your worldview.

"One man was very angry and said to me, 'I hate your God! I don't believe he exists!' I could have glibly answered, 'How can you hate something that doesn't exist? Who are you angry at?' What I actually said to him was, 'Why are you so angry? Why does this question mean so much to you?' He replied, 'God killed my wife.' My response was, 'Really? God killed your wife? Who told you that?' 'Some Christians told me that it was God's will that my wife died.' I told him God isn't someone who is playing dice, a cosmic chess player and we are just pawns in his game. I said, 'Can I ask you some questions? What did your wife die of?' 'Cancer.' 'OK, why is there cancer in the world?' 'I don't know.' 'If there was no God, would there still be cancer in the world?' 'Yes.' So I said I wanted to pose two questions: why is there cancer in the world and what does God do about it?"

No easy answers

Sometimes people ask, "How can there be a God who is love if he allows suffering?" That comes back again to the question of how we understand suffering. There isn't always a direct equation. If I get drunk and walk out into the road and get hit by a car, that's my fault. But if I have cancer, that might not be my fault. It may not be because of anything that I have done. There isn't necessarily that direct link.

Biblical perspectives

The book of Job is important for Christians because people around Job were not really asking, "Why does God allow suffering?" but, "What has God actually done about it?" The "Why" question was never really answered for Job.

Does God care that we suffer? In answer to that question, we can assert that we know God cares because nobody suffered more than Jesus. Also, there is going to be a world, as described in Revelation 7, where there will be no more tears, no more sin and suffering, and so on.

We can also emphasise personal experience and history. Western, middle-class liberals will often ask about the question of suffering because they picture God as a kind of Disney figure – one who is always going to give them exactly what they want. That's the God they've been brought up to believe in – a kind of sugar daddy in the sky. But that's not the God who exists. That's not the God of the Bible.

One of the intriguing things about the problem of suffering is that in countries where there is a significantly high degree of suffering, far more people believe in God than in countries where life is comparatively easier. Why is that? Why are there far more people in Haiti or on the African continent who believe in God? Are you going to be a racist and say it's because they are ignorant? Maybe it's because of their suffering. Maybe that's one of the reasons. Maybe suffering points us towards God.

If you want some help, C. S. Lewis's *The Problem of Pain* is brilliant for the theory, and his *A Grief Observed* is brilliant for the practice, because there he wrote about the death of his wife.

Why are you such a homophobe?

This is a big issue in Western Europe and possibly elsewhere too. The question is usually, "What do you think of homosexuality?" but it normally translates as, "Why are you such a homophobe?"

It is a mistake to answer that question directly and straight away. What you have to do is work out where the question is coming from.

There are several points to stress, and you can adapt them to your situation.

"In the Borders bookshop in Glasgow I was giving a talk on God and science. At the end, the manager stood up and said, 'What do you think of homosexuality?' I joked and said, 'You're not supposed to ask questions. You're the manager.' He didn't even want me there, and he glowered at me, so I looked at him again and said, 'OK. Are you asking me that as a question? Are you really concerned and you want to know what I think about homosexuality? Or are you making an accusation, are you asking me why I'm such a homophobe?' He said to me, 'Oh, it's the latter. I'm asking you why you are such a homophobe?' So I said to him, 'Well that's unfair because you don't know me. My talk has been about God and science, and I'm really inclined not to answer your question. However, out of courtesy, I will . . . on one condition.' He said, 'What's that?' I said, 'That you answer my question.' He said, 'OK.' I said, 'Are there any forms of sexuality that you would consider

> to be wrong?' He thought for a second, and said, 'You clever so-and-so. If I say No, you're going to ask about bestiality or paedophilia. But if I say Yes, you're going to ask me how I know?' I said to him, 'I'm not the only clever so-and-so here because that is exactly what I was going to do. You're right.' Then I said, 'But now, because you've answered my question, I'll answer yours, and then we are leaving it'."

Homophobia is wrong

Homophobia is silly, sinful and wrong. A Christian does not need to be afraid of anyone. There may be homophobes within the church but there are probably many more homophobes outwith the church. Homophobia is wrong – full stop.

God's truth

There is a God and he has revealed himself to us in his Word.

He created us and we should follow the Maker's instructions. He created us male and female equally in his image. And as part of that he ordained marriage to be between a man and a woman. He also created us to be sexual beings and his instructions are clear: sex should be within marriage between one man and one woman and sex outwith that context is wrong.

Believing these things does not make us homophobes. Many people today dismiss such views; they have grown up in a culture where it's the norm to have many partners. Our concern is not with the sexuality but with the context – sexual relations should be enjoyed within marriage, marriage between one man and one woman. Western society has been based on that understanding of marriage for 2000 years; it has served us well and to change that would be entirely wrong. To say that people who hold these views are necessarily homophobic is itself bigoted and intolerant.

The other thing about the issue of homosexuality is the question about identity. What would we say to a gay rights activist who spoke about his experience of 'coming out' in school, being bullied and rejected by the church. We should assure him of a welcome, and point out that we are talking at different levels. He would say that his identity is that he is homosexual. Our perspective is not that we are heterosexual and he is homosexual. We believe that our identity is firstly that we are human beings, created in God's image; after that come things like being a husband, being a father, being Scottish. These are all key parts of our identity (for some of us!). We don't say that sexuality is not part of people's identity but that it is not so important as they suggest. When you bring up this issue of identity you're walking into a minefield – but then again this whole question of homosexuality is a minefield.

So, answer it coherently; this is one question that shouldn't be answered aggressively. Answer it compassionately. Don't deviate or stray from the Bible. The minute you do, you are going to be tied into knots.

Why not believe in "The Flying Spaghetti Monster"?

In Christian circles, there are books and courses that are formulaic – e.g. *10 things to say to Jehovah's Witnesses*. Well, the new atheists have similar things. Sometimes you get asked questions that people think are very funny – for example, "Why don't you believe in the flying spaghetti monster?" This is an attempt to make fun of our claims that faith is evidence-based; the "flying spaghetti monster" story claims that there is no more evidence for the God of the Bible than there is for such a flying spaghetti monster or, as Bertrand Russell put it, for a chocolate teapot orbiting the earth.

What they're really saying is that you can't disprove it but you can't prove it either. What is the answer to that? Be aggressive with this one because the questioner thinks s/he is being really clever when in reality s/he is being idiotic.

One simple point to make is this: *"If you or any of your mentors like Richard Dawkins, Christopher Hitchens, etc, think that the flying spaghetti monster is so important why haven't you written books about it? Why? Simply because nobody believes in it. If you're saying that belief in the flying spaghetti monster is equivalent to belief in God, what you are really saying is that believers are complete idiots. That's not an argument – it's mere personal abuse."*

Proof and evidence

You can then get into the subject of the nature of proof. What do people mean by proof? What do they mean when they ask for proof of God's existence? When someone asks you for proof, you need to expand the context of the discussion. There are things that we all believe which we cannot prove. Can you prove that there are other minds than your own? Can you prove that you didn't come into existence, complete with all your memories, yesterday? How could you prove such things? Actually, you could argue that the only things that are really capable of being proved are in the field of mathematics – certain formulas and so on.

This is coming back to presuppositions because what's happening here is that people are presupposing:

- That they can determine what proof is
- That they themselves are capable of judging what the evidence means
- That it's their experience that counts

We presuppose different things:

- That there is order in the universe
- That there is a creator

We don't dispute that evidence is important but none of us is neutral. Therefore none of us is able to check that evidence completely independently.

The President of a university Atheist Society once said, "Even if you could prove that there is a God, I wouldn't worship him!" In that one phrase he summarised why all the evidence in the world wouldn't do any good to convince him.

You can never convince anyone completely with evidence but you can never convince them without evidence either.

"I was speaking at the Faclan Book Festival in Stornoway, and Richard Dawkins turned up and asked a question. My argument was that I don't like flying but I boarded the plane to fly to the island of Lewis. I didn't know and couldn't prove how the engine would work. I didn't know the principles of it. I couldn't build an engine. I wasn't a pilot. I couldn't fly a plane. There were many things I couldn't prove. I couldn't prove that the plane would not crash and so on. But I reasoned that this plane had flown many times, that the pilot was properly trained, that it was a reputable company, that I'd gone through this before, that there were thousands of other planes in the sky, that if the weather was really bad the Met office would report it and air traffic control would not allow the flight. After reasoning all these things, in faith I got on that plane. Richard Dawkins' response to that was, 'Yes but that's not like belief in God. That's belief based upon evidence and on experience.' To which my response was, 'Professor Dawkins, that's exactly it. Our belief in God is belief based upon evidence.' There is plenty of evidence for God. There is not absolute proof because there is not absolute proof for anything. But there is plenty of evidence. In the back of *The Dawkins Letters* I listed 10 evidences for God. When Francis Collins of the Human Genome Project was converted, he was won over by C.S. Lewis's argument that the greatest evidence was the moral law of the universe and the moral law within us. I think the concept of morality, beauty, creation, Jesus Christ, the Scriptures, the church, the very fact that we can conceive of a God, all these different things offer plenty of evidence for God."

Aren't religions evil?

The way to answer this question is not to become immediately defensive and say things like, *"But I'm not religious. I'm Christian."*

You could simply avoid the question by saying *"What do you mean by evil? What's your concept of evil? It's from religion that we get the concept of evil. So what do you mean by evil? I can't answer your question unless you can tell me what you mean by evil?"*

You could answer the question by saying, *"No, religions aren't evil; human beings are evil and it's human beings who invent religion"*. Man-made religions are idols, and they do a great deal of harm. There are things done in the name of religion, including Christianity, that are evil. Even genuine, biblical, born-again believers will sometimes do things that are evil. If people say (*á la* Daniel Dennett, Richard Dawkins) that the world is divided into good people and bad people, and good people do good things whereas bad people do bad things, but for good people to do bad things it takes religion, then their view of the world is incredibly naïve, wrong and twisted. And their view of religion is just as ignorant.

"Religion" covers so many different things that you cannot possibly equate all religions. The difference between biblical Christianity and religion is this: in every religion in the world, mankind reaches up to God, but in biblical Christianity, God reaches down to mankind. You can say to people, *"Yes, religious people can do harm, and Yes, religions can do harm, just as you can take anything good and you can use it for something that is evil. So I want to talk about Someone who comes to free us from all evil, including religious evil, and to enable us to know Jesus Christ".*

Questions for further study, discussion and action

Consider how you would answer each of the questions discussed in this chapter in ways that would be culturally appropriate to your context:

- Hasn't science disproved God?

- How can there be a God who is love if he allows suffering?

- Why are you such a homophobe?

- Why not believe in "The Flying Spaghetti Monster"?

- Aren't religions evil?

Are there other questions that people in your cultural context are asking? If so, what are they and how would you answer them?

Chapter 7

Epilogue

Quench-type events are not some kind of new, foolproof, sure-fire way of making your church grow with new converts. It is not a one-size-fits-all, memorized-script approach. Rather, Quench events are designed to encourage and provoke Christians to reach out beyond the walls of the church building/meeting place, to places where people gather daily – cafés, pubs, and other places known for social gathering. Quench events are designed to utilize the café culture as a bridge for a reasonable persuasive presentation of the gospel.

This booklet has outlined a process and guidelines needed to facilitate a Quench event in a local venue. It is not designed as a step-by-step instruction booklet such as one would find in assembling a piece of recently purchased IKEA furniture. Unlike an IKEA assembly manual that must be followed meticulously, the success of a Quench event requires that any church or Christian organisation that desires to 'persuasively evangelise' through a Quench-type event *will* need to determine the best way to incorporate the principles found in the booklet into its own cultural context.

Not all events will require a professional or high-powered "apologist". Sometimes the presence of such a "professional apologist" could even cause the event to become too large and so lose the warmth and character that a small group offers for discussion and dialogue. Nevertheless, a Quench-type event will require the speaker or performer to possess a certain expertise in his/her field. We would hardly expect an amateur stargazer, who is fascinated with the heavens and owns a small, albeit powerful, telescope and boasts of a handful of books on constellations, to be able to explain everything about the origins of the universe!

However, the Christian church is not devoid of trained, professional scientists, biologists, economists, and the like, who are more than capable of relating their expertise to their personal faith. Pastors, leaders, elders, missionaries – find those people in your church (or invite them from other churches) and encourage them to use their talents and training to give a reasonable presentation of the gospel in an invigorating, yet relaxed environment.

It is not that Quench events need to revolve around intellectual, scientific or theological pursuits. Be creative. What about interpretive dance? Or gardening, relating the magnificent details of each rose petal or unique European arbutus to the design of the One who created the first garden. Would a thirty minute talk work in your culture, comparing the lyrics of three of four rap groups or hip hop artists, inquiring about the message communicated, asking what effects these messages may have on the listeners? (Of course, use

Christian rap and hip hop artists in the comparison).

Quench events are designed to reach twenty-first century people in their own cultural context, creating an event in a familiar, non-threatening, relaxed atmosphere that should be fun. For example:

- a marketing analyst desires to invite his colleague to a discussion on capitalism, socialism and Christian values, but doesn't want him to be bombarded with religious jargon.

- a daughter-in-law believes her mother-in-law would be interested in a conversation on her favourite hobby, sponsored by her church which is hosting the next Quench event.

- a taxi driver has a genuine desire to share the gospel with his customers. He made a special friend who is now a repeat customer and he would like to invite him to hear a testimony of a local, respected politician. The event is sponsored by his church, but held in the local pub.

- a heart surgeon-in-residence has a growing respect for her mentor, who she knows would never attend a church service. Maybe she would come to a stimulating discussion about her speciality area of interest if it were held in a café.

The apostle Paul spoke about his commitment to use "all possible means" to bring people to the Saviour (1 Corinthians 9:22). It is in this spirit that the Solas team presents this booklet, with the prayer that the Lord Himself will bless it as we seek to fulfil His great commission to make disciples in the strength of His great promise to be with His people always (Matthew 28:19-20).